CLOSE ENCOUNTERS
WITH DONALD TRUMP

By Scoop Malinowski

Cover Art by Karin Billings

CONTRIBUTORS

John Lloyd
Mike Tyson
John McEnroe
Randy Gordon
Paul Vaden
Lynn Quayle
Dana White
Kenneth Lundgren
Larry Holmes
Ray Collins
Steve Lott
Chuck Wepner
George Foreman
Heidi Albertsen
Ann Grossman
Joe Wolfer
Tiger Woods
Johan Kriek
Jackie Kallen
Bernie Nicholls
Bernie Dillon
John Scully
Isaac Oyedele
Benjamin Clarke
Pat English
Rick Glaser
Dan C. Weil

Melvin Stanley
Andrew Golota
Jim Tarsy
Mario Costa
Jimmy Murray
Chris Kotsopolous
Roscoe Tanner
Barry Beck
Michael Marley
Gary Cohn
Larry Barnes
Randy Walker
Joe Abba
Nick Kish
Iran Barkley
Chris Alderucci
Randy Neumann
Vijay Amritraj
Vinny Pazienza
Kirk Lang
Lloyd Carroll
Bobby Czyz
Carling Bassett-Seguso
Jeff Freeman
Dave Kozlowski
Montell Griffin
Liz Crokin

CLOSE ENCOUNTERS
WITH DONALD TRUMP

This book has nothing to do with politics or agendas. The original vision for this book was very simple. It is simply a collection of memories and anecdotes from a wide range of fifty-two people who have had close encounters with the current President of the United States of America, Donald Trump. That is all this book is about, nothing more, nothing less.

Let's start with my two close encounters with Trump. The first...I was on summer break in college in 1988, living on Long Beach Island working my own business as a self-employed auto detailer, literally going door to door to hustle business. During that summer I kept busy by also attending professional boxing events an hour south in Atlantic City, courtesy of a media credential I managed to wangle for my college (Kean) newspaper (The

Independent), even though school was not in session during summer. One of the first boxing shows I ever attended in AC with a media credential was on June 25, 1988 at the Trump Plaza hotel and casino, featuring WBC Featherweight champion Azumah Nelson of Ghana, Africa, defending against Lupe Suarez. Sitting at ringside in press row, I noticed directly across the ring was Donald Trump himself. During the fight, we made eye contact a couple of times, presumably because Trump saw me as a curiosity - I stood out as ringside press row as a 22-year-old, the youngest by far of all the other reporters. Nelson defended the title that afternoon by TKO. The fight was broadcast by ABC. Two days later on Monday June 27, Trump helped promote one of the biggest fights of the decade - Mike Tyson vs Michael Spinks, which ended sensationally in a first-round knockout.

The next time I saw Trump in person was ten years later at the US Open, inside Louis Armstrong Stadium in 1998. It was a night match featuring the world's second-best player Marcelo Rios of Chile against an Italian journeyman named Giorgio Galimberti. Rios won the first set 6-2 but lost his concentration in the second set and dropped the tiebreaker 7-4. That's precisely when Trump arrived to the stadium, by the same corner of the arena that regular fans enter. He strides down the walkway with his female companion during the break, as both of the court combatants sat at their chairs, calculating their next moves for the third set. When Trump entered Louie Armstrong, the stadium crowd noticed his presence and expressed a slight buzz, a reaction which arrested the attention of Rios. Rios spotted Trump in the audience and saw him walk to his seat. Rios surely realized Trump had abandoned a blowout match on Arthur Ashe Stadium and he was flattered that Trump went out of his way to see the controversial but supremely talented Chilean who had achieved the ATP no. 1 ranking earlier in the year in Miami when he defeated Andre Agassi.

The match resumed and Rios suddenly began to put on an electrifying show, undoubtedly sparked and inspired by the unexpected visit from Trump. Rios took over the match and dominated with a sensational display of his best tennis after a lackluster effort in the second set. Rios also showed uncustomary extra passion and fire to Trump, which he rarely showed in the majority of his matches. Rios made gestures like hissing his tongue at Galimberti's missed shots and colorfully celebrating his own brilliant play. Without a doubt, Trump awakened the best of Rios, who went on to pummel the outclassed opponent, 6-2 and 6-2.

These are my two most memorable close encounters with Trump.

Fifty-two more people also kindly shared their own close encounters with Donald Trump...

Ronald Reagan: "For the life of me, and I'll never know how to explain it, when I met that man, I felt like I was the one shaking hands with The President."

John Lloyd (Former professional tennis player): "I've known Donald for many years. I've played tennis against him, played golf with him. I've had some fun times with Donald. A lot of people obviously dislike him. He's always been very nice to me. One funny memory that I've had with him – he's brilliant at his clubs. He knows all of his members – there's 250 of them. He knows them all, exactly what they do. At Trump International in West Palm Beach, he knows their names and what they do. So what he does, when he's walking around the place, like at lunch, he's walking up to a table. Rather than just say, Hey how's it going guys, how are you? He'll come up to the table and say, This is Fred, king of the fast food restaurants. Or this one guy that owns a huge car dealership, and he'll say so and so owns the best car dealership in the world."

"With me, he always used to – which is kind of good for my ego – he'd call me the great John Lloyd, winner of three Grand Slams. Because I won three Grand Slams in mixed doubles you see (1982 Roland Garros, 1983 and 1984 Wimbledon, all with Wendy Turnbull). And he would always say it. And one time I was there with my sister from England, she was visiting with my brother-in-law. And then we were sitting at a table. And Mr.

Trump was sitting over there. And I say to my sister, There's Donald Trump over there. She kind of looks over at him and all that. And Trump comes up and blind sides – I didn't see him coming. And all the sudden, he stands right here and we're sitting there and he looks at my sister and he points to me...'The great John Lloyd, winner of three Grand Slam titles.' And I said, 'Donald, she knows. It's my sister!' And he went off. 'Oh, have a nice day!' I completely changed his rhythm. Because he wasn't expecting it. And we laugh about it. I'm writing a book (Dear John) which will be published next year. That story will be in my book. There's a chapter about him in it."

Question: Can you share your analysis of the Donald Trump golf and tennis games?

John Lloyd: "Well, golf, he's bloody good. I've played with him maybe four or five times. He always has the joke, he says, 'John, I'm glad you were a pretty good tennis player because you're a shitty golfer [laughs]!' And he's right, I'm a shitty golfer. He's always been fun with me. He's the quickest golfer of all time. I mean, there's like no practice swings. He wants to hit and move. He plays the round in like two hours. So with him, it's like you're kind of flustered. You get to the ball and he's looking. You've got to hit this. There's no, like, warm-up routine. if Rafael Nadal was the same in golf like he is in tennis (Nadal is a notoriously slow player, with methodical routines before each point), they'd have a big fight in five minutes. That kind of thing. But he's a very good golfer."

"Tennis - he wasn't bad. I don't know if he's playing now. I played against him at a couple of events. I'll tell you one thing about him, he was pretty brave because he used to stand right on top of the net and volley. And he'd be playing against pros. And they would hit him. And he'd stand there and take more. He got hit a few times. He would not back off. He just stood there. That's the way he knew he had a chance. He knew if he moved back, they would get at him. He wasn't bad but he wasn't as good as the pros. And he would stand there and try and swat the ball away. He got hit a few times and just sucked it up and came back for more [laughs]. So, put it this way, he's a better golfer than tennis player."

Dunlop

Mike Tyson (Former Heavyweight Champion): "Listen, I'm a black motherfucker from the poorest town in the country (Brownsville in Brooklyn, NY). I've been through a lot in life. And I know Donald Trump. When I see him, he shakes my hand and respects my family. None of them, Barack, whoever, nobody else does that. They're gonna be who they are and disregard me and my family. So I'm voting for him. If I can get 200,000 people or more to vote for him, I'm gonna do it."

"Trump, Trump, Trump, Trump, Trump, Trump, Trump, Trump, Trump, Trump! You vote for Trump; you get the bump. I like who I like. I am not registered (democrat or republican) for shit. This is what I think should happen. I know Trump. Nobody else who's running for President is gonna shake my hand and do anything kind for me. I'm a bad nigger to them. I don't look good around these democrat guys or republican guys or those who are politically inclined. I made a lot of money (from Trump in my fights in Atlantic City). I made a lot of money when I had a republican president."

"I was going to keep my opinion to myself. I'm voting for Trump. This is my opinion. This is what I like. This is what I believe. If I like Donald Trump and am gonna vote for him, so what? What are you gonna do? Shoot me or beat me up? I don't think so."

Mike Tyson drawing by Bud Boccone.

John McEnroe (Tennis Champion): "I've known Donald Trump a little over the years. Donald Trump put $1,000,000 on the table for a winner take all tennis match between me and Serena Williams. At least he didn't bear a grudge when I turned down the offer. My dad sent Trump a letter of support asking if there was anything, he could do to help at the start of his campaign to get the Republican nomination for the 2016 presidential election. Of course, at that point, no one thought Trump had a chance of winning the election."

"Trump has had a box right next to the broadcaster's booth at the US Open ever since the Arthur Ashe Stadium opened (in 1997). Even before he became President, you didn't see him there as much as he used to be, it's a sign of tennis losing popularity that Donald's not around to get his mug on TV. But at the 2015 US Open he was very much in attendance and Mike Tirico - one of the best play-by-play guys on ESPN before he moved to NBC - said, 'You know Trump, right? Let's go over and say hello,' because he wanted to meet him."

"Patty (his wife) and Ava (daughter) were with me and they were telling me, 'Don't you dare go over there. He's a misogynist and a blowhard, it could hurt your reputation.' But I said, 'Hey, come on, it's no big deal.' So I took Mike over and sure enough, ESPN showed it on TV, me hugging Donald like we were long lost brothers or something. Trump did seem more pleased to see me than he usually would be and I only realized why when he started saying, 'John, thank you so much for the letter your wrote. I've already got it up on the wall in my office.' I hoped this was fake news because I didn't want everyone who went into Donald Trump's office during the election thinking I was his number one fan. Now that Donald has been elected President of the United States, there might be an ambassadorship in this for me.

(From McEnroe's 2017 book "John McEnroe: But Seriously" (Little, Brown and Company.)

John McEnroe painting by Karin Billings.

Randy Gordon (Former Ring Magazine Editor-in-Chief): "I met Donald Trump several times throughout the 1980's and 1990's, but two dates stand out in my mind. The first was on Wednesday, October 17,1984. My youngest daughter, Greer, had been born six days earlier. I left the morning of the 16th to announce a televised fight the night before in Atlantic City, then stayed over for a morning breakfast meeting with Donald Trump in Trump Plaza. As Editor-in-Chief of The Ring, I was interviewing Trump for the cover story in the following month's Ring. I had intended to put Trump on the cover. The interview went very well, with Trump telling me, '...that was the most in-depth interview I have ever given.' He was very respectful throughout the interview, telling me I could come back as his guest to Trump Plaza any time I wanted, simply by calling his personal assistant, whom he would speak to later that morning."

"In the early afternoon, Ring's staff photographer, Jack Goodman, would be showing up to do a photo shoot with Trump, as the cover story would also feature him on the cover. I'll always believe the magazine would have been a huge seller, just the way Ring's 'Howard Cosell cover' did record sales around four years

earlier. We never got to find out. When I returned to
Ring the next morning, I saw former Editor-in-Chief
Nat Loubet sitting at a desk. Nat had been retired from
the magazine for close to a year. Why was he there
now? He told me to sit down. He had bad news for
me. While I was in Atlantic City, Ring's three owners—
Dave DeBusschere, Nick Kladis and Jim Bukata—had
come in to do some 'house-cleaning.'"

"A few heads were going to roll, as well as a few of
their other minor publications, including Boxing
Illustrated and its editor, Nigel Collins. However, doing
a great job in saving his job, Collins said it should be me
who should be fired, as I was going out of town nearly
every week for TV assignments, and that I was in
Atlantic City as they spoke. Of course, he didn't tell
them I was interviewing Donald Trump for next
month's cover, and they bought his story. My days at
The Ring ended that day, with Collins going on to run
the magazine for the next twenty years or so, and me
heading into television, the New York State Athletic
Commission and back into radio and TV."

"The next time I interviewed Trump was on February
8, 1988, I was in Atlantic City's Convention Center,
doing blow-by-blow on a televised card which featured

Roberto Duran against Ricky Stackhouse. My color analyst was the great Gil Clancy. During a break in the card, which featured not only Duran, but Mark Breland and Marlon Starling, as well, my producer told us in our headsets that Donald Trump would be walking in soon and be seated behind us. He told us, 'Mr. Trump will be brought over to you at the end of this fight and Randy, you'll do a one-on-one interview with him.'"

"When Trump was brought to ringside after the fight by two large bodyguards, a chair was placed next to me and I pointed to a set of headphones. Trump put them on. After the decision was announced, I heard my producer say in my ear, 'Okay, Randy, bring in Donald Trump.'"

"...Joining us now at ringside is 'Mr. Atlantic City' himself, casino owner and boxing aficionado, Mr. Donald Trump."

"As he began to speak, he did so in a deep, gravelly voice, in a speaking intonation as if he was imitating a WWE wrestler.

"'Listen here, Gordon...' he began. Then we both laughed and got into the interview, talking about

Atlantic City as a hotbed for boxing, which it was, at that time. I know this was much longer than you wanted, but I have never spoken at length about my interviews with the man who would become, a few decades and change later, the 45th President of the United States. I may just have to expand on this and turn it into a chapter in my next boxing book, 'Glove Story.'"

The RING
SINCE 1922
OVER A THOUSAND
RESULTS IN
EVERY ISSUE
JULY 1988
USA: $2.25
CANADA: $2.75
UK: £1.85 47855
EVERLAST
EXCLUSIVE INTERVIEW
WITH DONALD TRUMP
SPECIAL
TYSON- SPINKS
PREVIEW ISSUE

Paul "The Ultimate" Vaden (Former boxing champion): "I met Donald Trump three times. At Trump Castle in 1994 when I fought there against Jason Papillon, at Trump Tower in 1995 when I was in New York for a press conference and in November of 1999 at the Taj Mahal in Atlantic City. He was ringside at the fight when I fought Stephan Johnson (which ended tragically with Johnson passing away from head injuries suffered in the bout). He complimented me on my boxing skills and hand speed. That individual was a huge boxing fan. In the hallway of my dressing room after the Stephan fight is where we talked. Everything was a blur so I don't remember anything in specific from him or anyone for that matter."

TRUMP
TAJ MAHAL
CASINO RESORT

Lynn Quayle (Former personal assistant to artist LeRoy Neiman): "When LeRoy and I would encounter Donald Trump in those early years, he was quite reserved and when he was married to Ivana he would let her carry the conversation at a large round dinner table prior to the boxing matches. He started to be more overt after his board game was released. We didn't see him much after Ivana and he divorced."

Dana White (CEO of Ultimate Fighting Championships): "When we first bought this company (UFC), no venues would even take us. Arenas around the world refused to host our events. Donald Trump was the first guy to say, 'We'll do the fights here.' Trump gave us our first shot over at Taj Mahal (in Atlantic City, November 2000, Randy Couture vs Kevin Randleman main event), and then we did two more events the next year. Then when we left and went to a bigger arena at The Meadowlands, he was one of the first guys there in his seat. Nobody took us seriously – nobody except Donald Trump. Donald was the first guy that recognized the potential that we saw in the UFC and encouraged us to build our business."

"I've been in the fight business my whole life. I know fighters. Donald Trump is a fighter, and I know he'll fight for this country."

"In my opinion, you can really tell a person's true character when they're happy for somebody else's success."

Question: How was it planned for Trump to attend the UFC event at Madison Square Garden in November 2019?

Dana White: "We had dinner last Thursday at the White House, and he said 'I'm coming. I'm coming to New York'. And I was like 'Oh my God! That's going to be a rough one! Why don't we do Vegas on the 14th (December)? And New York was the only one that he could do, so he came tonight."

"They (Secret Service) wanted him in a suite, of course, (but) he doesn't listen to them. He does what he wants to do. But yeah, they wanted him in a suite. I'm not an expert in security, but I think it's a lot easier to protect him in a suite than it is in the second row. But, again, testament to our fans. It's our President. It's the President of the United States, man. And tonight, I was happy and proud that the crowd here in New York treated him with respect and just made the night so much cooler. Everything was so cool tonight."

189
BUD
LIGHT
McGRE
GM
AND

Kenneth Lundgren (Elite Endurance Cycling coach and writer): "I was at UFC 244 for the Masvidal-Diaz fight, big production in Madison Square Garden, early November 2019, fight night and a grand Saturday evening. I had purchased really, really nice seats, the first section back from the floor, still very close to the Octagon – in my humble opinion, these were the best seats in the entire house, had clean view of every part of the arena. UFC noted Donald Trump was going to spectate, this had been the news, he was coming to watch the main event for special BMF belt (Bad Motherfucker), The Rock was going to put the BMF belt on winner – it was a big deal."

"Just before 10 pm, I could hear a murmur building in the crowd and to the left, where fighters were making their entrance to the Octagon, a small group appeared, slowly walking down aisle, into the heart of arena. Yes, Donald Trump and his entourage – Secret Service out the ying-yang, on the perimeter and covering all corners, points-of-entry. It was an impressive production."

"The President of the United States walked towards his section amidst a raising level of boos and cheers. Both sounds were present, the jeers louder than the clapping and whistling. Trump was in no rush, oblivious, smiling and waving president-like to random parts of the crowd as he approached his section. His 'section' was three or four complete rows cageside, to the left of the Octagon – primetime awesome seats. The UFC was showing much respect by giving the President this much real estate on arguably the hottest event of the year. Dana White, the president of the UFC, was sitting just off to his right – these were the top seats in the house, and the President had thirty to forty seats reserved for his company."

"The President and his group took their seats. It looked like a party in that section, everyone laughing, smiling, shaking hands, hugging, whooping it up – clearly these people were loving the energy of fight night and Madison Square Garden! The energy was uncanny, the audience was definitely alive – whether you love or hate the President, you certainly feel a certain way towards him, and you felt that way now, as did everyone else."

"About an hour later, before the main event, Dana White made his way over to Trump's section and Trump got to his feet – to a rousing ovation. With his first appearance, certainly a harsh mix of cheers and angry boos could be heard. But, in this second coming, the crowd boomed and beamed with approval – Madison Square Garden and the UFC audience were cheering loudly for the President of the United States."

"Trump stood in place, hand up and waving like a king as he turned to view different parts of the crowd."

Larry Holmes (Former World Heavyweight Champion): "My first memory of Donald Trump is when I tried to talk to him. At one of the hotels down there in Atlantic City. We were in the lobby. I walked up to him (and said), 'Hey Donald. How are you?' He looked at me like I was a piece of shit. So I don't care for Donald Trump. That's Donald Trump. He's the man. It's all about him. If it's not about him, it isn't about nothing. Life goes on."

Ray Collins (News anchor ABC affiliate in Sarasota, FL): "It was the mid-1990s, I was anchoring the TV news for the CBS affiliate in Buffalo—and my then-girlfriend and I took a trip to Manhattan for a weekend away. Part of our plans was to see "Phantom of the Opera" on Broadway."

"Shortly after we arrived at the Pantages Theater, I was leaning against a wall waiting for Jodi in the ladies' room when a couple walked toward us with a similar arrangement. She went into the ladies' room while he stood next to me outside. I recognized him instantly. Donald Trump. At the time, he had a development proposal for a casino project in Buffalo—so that was my 'in.' 'Hey, I think your timing for that casino in Buffalo is perfect, they need jobs there,' I began. 'Oh yeah? What do you do?' he quickly shot back. "

"I'm a TV news anchor," I replied.

"You look like one," he deadpanned.

"After a little more talk about the project, our respective dates emerged almost simultaneously and seamlessly the four of us were walking toward our seats together which wound up being nearly side by side. I don't recall who his date was—but it wasn't any of his current or former wives. At intermission, he and I walked out side by side and I resumed a conversation. 'Do you like the musical?' I asked. 'Oh yeah, love it, I've seen it several times,' he said. I had recently read Swim with the Sharks and Don't Get Eaten Alive, and Author Harvey McKay talked about the value of seizing moments, or 'swinging for the fences,' when they present themselves."

"Who helps you with your media?" I heard myself ask.

"What do you mean?" he said.

"Who teaches you how to do better TV interviews, soundbites, etc.?" I continued.

"Nobody. Why?" he replied.

"We're in New York for the weekend, why don't we have breakfast tomorrow morning and I'll pass along some tips," I offered.
"I'm playing golf in the morning, but I like your style," he said.

"I later sent a letter to him, telling him I'd be willing to come back to New York at any time to help, but I didn't get a response."

"Fast forward twenty years, it's now mid-2015 and I'm working for the ABC-TV station in Sarasota, Florida. Trump was coming to town to receive an award from the Sarasota County Republican Party as 'Statesman of the Year.' It was his second time winning the award in the past five years, but this visit had more intrigue as rumors were swirling that he was close to announcing his plans to run for President."

"There were only about four or five reporters present, and I was the only affiliate TV station. When Trump finally arrived—very late—he posed for pictures with supporters but saw my ABC microphone and began to cultivate me, with repeated eye contact and nods. After a group interview, I approached him one-on-one and said, 'You and I have actually met before.' He said, 'Oh yeah, where?' 'It was at Pantages Theater twenty years ago, we were there to see 'Phantom of the Opera'...I asked you to have breakfast the next morning to talk about media tips and you said you were golfing but you liked my style,' I recounted."

"Without skipping a beat, he said, 'You haven't changed a bit - I still like your style."

"With that, he turned to an event photographer and said, 'Get a picture with this guy, he's great.' As a reporter I felt a little self-conscious posing with the person I came to cover—and I winced when I saw him hold a 'thumbs up' in front of me. I was fully aware he was massaging me for good coverage."

"That was our last contact - but that wasn't the last I heard from his team that night. I had given my card to his press person, Hope Hicks, who later called me as they were heading back to the airport. She asked if I could give her a copy of our interview. I explained the station has a policy against that, and it usually requires a court-order. She hung up and my experience with Team Trump was over."

"Weeks later, he announced his plans for President...my station sent me to Cleveland to cover the Republican National Convention...I never got near him...and the rest is history."

"As I watch him now as President, I've often thought of offering him my media tips, knowing that he seems to like my style."

Steve Lott (Las Vegas Boxing Hall of Fame founder): "Trump teamed up with Robin Givens to pull Mike Tyson away from Bill Cayton. Trump is a great con man. He quickly realized that Robin was a con artist too. Trump knew that Robin lied to Mike about being pregnant just to get Mike to marry her. Trump gave Robin complete access to his lawyers and accountants to try to dump Cayton. When Trump's accountants found out that Bill and Jim Jacobs overpaid Mike, it ruined Robin's plans. At the same time Don King was making his move on Mike. King gave Mike a promotional contract to sign. When Robin read it she realized Don would be able to steal all the money. She knew there can be only one thief in the family – and that was going to be her. So, she re-signed with Cayton knowing that all the fighter's money would be going to Mike. And then she could steal it."

Question: Any personal memories of Trump?
Steve Lott: "Actually yes, in a way. My buddy was the guy who brought Marla Maples to New York. He was also Trump's bodyguard. When Trump saw Marla he asked my buddy if it's Ok to go after her. My buddy said yes, figuring it would get him closer to Trump. While she and Trump were dating behind Ivana's back, Marla

called me to go out. I passed since she was (bleeping) Trump and it felt sleazy."

Chuck Wepner (Former World Heavyweight Title challenger and the inspiration for the film "Rocky"): "Yes I know Trump. He invited me down to Mar A Lago. He loved the fighters. I was there years before he became president. He was interested in promoting a cage fight, me with Tex Cobb. But it never happened. He couldn't pay me enough money (smiles). But I like Trump. Between you and me, Bayonne (NJ) is a democrat town. But I like Trump. He's doing a good job. I like what he's doing and the economy is doing good."

Chuck Wepner painting by Mike Saviello.

George Foreman (Former World Heavyweight Champion): "I was broke too. Bankrupt. Trump was part of writing those checks so I could be on the wealthy side again. So, I 'll always be grateful to the entrepreneur Donald Trump. And now President Donald Trump. He's a good president. A lot of people don't like him but evidently more do, because he was elected President of the United States."

FIGHT NIGHT AND MAIN EVENTS IN ASSOCIATION WITH TOP RANK AND THE MGM GRAND PRESENT
NOVEMBER 5, 1994
MOORER vs FOREMAN
WORLD HEAVYWEIGHT CHAMPIONSHIP
MGM GRAND

Heidi Albertsen (Model): "I respect and value my friendships with the Trumps. Because of this respect, I don't speak publicly about my friends and their private lives. I wish you the best, but please understand I cannot be a part of this book.

Ann Grossman (Former top 30 pro tennis player): " I was playing at the US Open in 1994, I played Arantxa Sanchez-Vicario the year she won the US Open. She beat Steffi Graf in the final. I lost to her on the centre court at the US Open, Louis Armstrong Stadium. And the next day I went out shopping in New York City. And I was across the street from Tiffany's and walking across. And I saw Donald Trump. We were on opposite sides of the street. And then he kept looking at me. I was looking at him. Because it was Donald Trump. And then he kept looking at me. Because we were passing by, walking by each other. And then he turned around and yelled, 'Hey Ann, that was a great match yesterday' It was in the round of 16 (Ann lost 62 60)."

NETPRO
Tour Star
Ann Grossman

Joe Wolfer (Financier): "He's smart but he's an egomaniac. And he's a bully. He's gotten away with all that over all the years and now he's finding out from the guys that he's dealing with now are probably as smart as he is, in a different way. But by and large, I'd still vote for him, in light of what's going on."

Question: How did you connect to do business with Trump?

Joe Wolfer: "I was in the finance business at a time when he needed some money. And I did business with him. And he handled himself well. I had no hard feelings with him. And I wish him the best because he's the President of our country. But he also should keep his mouth closed sometimes if he's not following a script."

Question: When was the deal? Details?

Joe Wolfer: "I owned a property that I took back from Bob Guccione of Penthouse Magazine. And I needed help in selling it. He recommended a broker for me which, unfortunately I didn't use. He was a little bit annoyed that I didn't use the broker that he recommended. But we had a good relationship. And it ended okay. He came on to better things, becoming the President of the United States."

Question: Lasting memory or anecdote of Donald Trump?

Joe Wolfer: "We never socialized. We met a few times. I met his prior wife, Marla Maples when her daughter was in her arms. And I looked at his beautiful apartment up on the top of Trump Tower, which was beautifully done. Those are my recollections. He's a unique person. But he's gotten away with his style of doing business he's done all his life and he's not changing now. Which he probably should adjust his lifestyle now because he's in a different arena."

TRUMP TOWER
TRUMP TOWER
GUCCI

Tiger Woods (Pro golfer): "Well, I've known Donald for a number of years. We've played golf together. We've had dinner together. I've known him pre-presidency and obviously during his presidency. He's the president of the United States. You have to respect the office. No matter who is in the office – you may dislike the personality or the politics – but we all must respect the office."

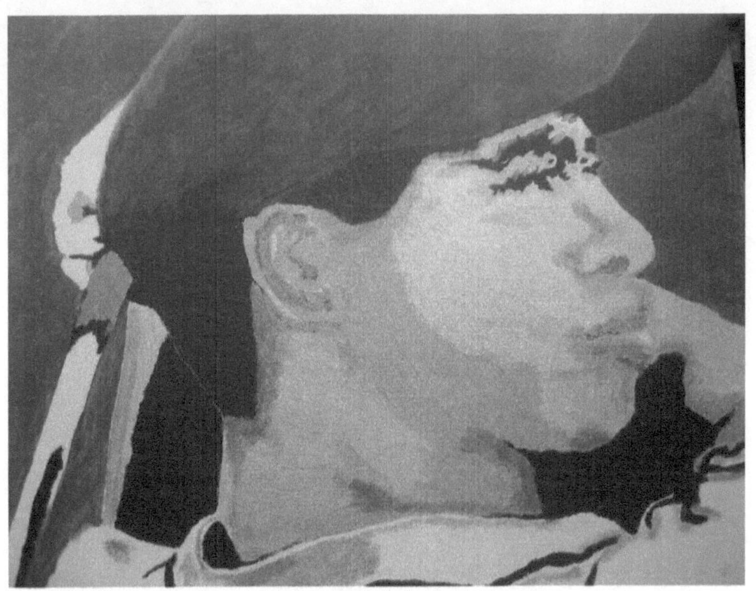

Tiger Woods painting by Scoop Malinowski.

Johan Kriek (Winner of two Australian Opens in tennis): "I met Donald Trump at Mar A Lago. I played doubles with him. And we won."

Question: How is his tennis game?

Johan Kriek: "What matters is WINNING [smiles]."

Jackie Kallen (Former boxing manager of James Toney and subject of the 2004 film "Against The Ropes"): "I have many memories of Donald Trump. My first encounter with him was the 1988 Mike Tyson - Michael Spinks fight. My ex-husband and I were with Thomas Hearns and his wife, and Bill Laimbeer (of the Detroit Pistons) and his wife. Donald and his then-wife Ivana hosted the most amazing party I have ever been to. The room was packed with A-listers including Jesse Jackson, Oprah Winfrey, Jack Nicholson, Warren Beatty, Billy Crystal, Herschel Walker, and so many others that you didn't know where to look first. Trump worked the room perfectly, greeting and shaking hands with all of his guests. He seemed approachable and extremely comfortable among this group of celebrities."

"A few years later, James Toney fought in Atlantic City at one of Trump's casinos (Trump Taj Mahal). Again, he was friendly, taking my ex-husband and I to dinner with his girlfriend Marla Maples. He gave us signed copies of "The Art of the Deal" and talked boxing and business."

"The only time that I saw Trump act unpleasant was after the Toney - (Dave) Tiberi fight. He was as warm and friendly as ever before the fight, but he disagreed loudly with the decision when Toney got the win (by judge's decision). He thought it was an outrage and went straight to Tiberi's locker room to console him. I remember him looking at me in the ring as the referee held Toney's hand in the air. He shook his head in disgust. Even though I had nothing to do with the decision, I could tell he was upset with me, and I did not know why. Not long after, a federal investigation into the fight was launched. They later concluded that there was no wrongdoing on anyone's part, but it led to the creation of the Muhammad Ali act."

TRUMP TOWER

Bernie Nicholls (Former NHL player for New York Rangers and Los Angeles Kings): Played in a golf event with him. Not bad, it was an event in New York when I was with the Rangers. It was in the 90's so it was no big deal that he was there because he wasn't nearly as popular then as he is now."

Question: How was his game?
Bernie Nicholls: "Not bad."

Bernie Dillon (Former executive with Trump Properties Atlantic City): "Donald Trump is a huge boxing fan, a huge sports fan. He gave us the opportunity to do incredible things in Atlantic City during his reign in Atlantic City. We had a lot of fun."

Question: Lasting memory of your years working for Donald Trump and his association with boxing?

Bernie Dillon: "He was at almost every fight. At almost every fight that he did he made time to come and sit ringside. I always remember him sitting with Muhammad Ali, with Oprah, Madonna, Paul Simon. He got the celebrities to come in. It was amazing."

Question: How did he become such a big boxing fan?

Bernie Dillon: "I think a lot of people our age, let's say anybody over fifty today grew up on boxing. Look at all the networks, ABC, NBC, CBS and then eventually ESPN and USA. There was boxing on national TV several nights a week. And we grew up on it. In the 70s all the big fights were on the networks before HBO started putting them on pay networks. It was a much bigger part of the sports scene at the time than it is today. I think we were all naturally – like we are football, basketball and baseball fans – we were boxing fans too."

Question: Do you remember him having any favorites?

Bernie Dillon: "Donald I think really enjoyed watching the little guys fight because they just gave their all. I remember one of the best fights we ever had, he was ecstatic ... the Roberto Duran-Iran Barkley fight (1989) – after a seventeen-inch snowstorm in Atlantic City. And those guys just went toe-to-toe for twelve rounds. We always said that was probably the best fight we had."

Question: What is your first memory of Donald?

Bernie Dillon: "It was at a boxing event. I was standing against the back wall at our old ballroom and he all the sudden was standing next to me and said, 'What do you think of this stuff? Does it really work for our casino?' He was learning. He was learning the casino business."

Question: That was when you were already working for him?

Bernie Dillon: "Well, we were Harrahs at Trump Plaza when we opened that property. So he was a partner to Harrahs. We, at that time, were all Harrahs employees. And he questioned us. I always remember that he listened to what people had to say."

John Scully (Professional boxer, trainer, TV analyst): "I have a picture from my encounter with Trump. I didn't speak to him but I was in Roy Jones dressing room the night he fought Vinny Pazienza in Convention Hall IN Atlantic City (June 1995). Derrick 'Smoke' Gainer fought on the undercard – he beat Harold Warren by decision to win the NABF Featherweight title – and Trump came in after the fight to congratulate Smoke. I saw that and I took a picture of it as it was happening. I thought it was pretty cool at that moment that he came back to the dressing room to congratulate an undercard fighter."

Isaac Oyedele (Artist from Nigeria):

Question: President Trump tweeting your artwork qualifies as a close encounter with Donald Trump. Can you share your point of view of the experience? Where were you when the President of the United States of America liked and retweeted your artwork of him?

Isaac Oyedele: "The experience for me has been mind blowing – for the US President to retweet, not only that but also took time to comment on my artwork as a Nigerian, makes that day almost unimaginable. I was at a brother's place when I saw a verified account 'Donald J. Trump' responding to me, I just ran out and hug everyone outside in excitement. 'You don't get the attention of Trump everyday,' one said."

Question: How has your life changed?

Isaac Oyedele: "Yes it has changed my life, gave me connections in more ways I could imagine."

Question: What inspired you to make a drawing of Trump in the first place?

Isaac Oyedele: "I love Trump for his appearance and speaking his mind – that in fact won him the Presidency. People can say what they say but you can't deny he is just the 'man.'"

Question: Can you talk about your new contacts and where in Nigeria are you from?

Isaac Oyedele: "I live in Osogbo, Osun State. My new contacts – not to sugarcoat – are basically potential clients and admirers. Celebrities and limelight figures don't like Trump so they wouldn't reach out. But anyways the golden retweet has lit my spirit ever since then – I feel like I could do anything."

@DOKS_ART
IG: @DOKS_ART

Benjamin Clarke (Attorney): "Not sure if it qualifies as an encounter, but I represented Mirage, the builder of the Borgata Hotel and Casino in Atlantic City, in the numerous lawsuits Trump filed to try to stop the Borgata's construction. This led to me spending an hour or so seated directly behind him in the Appellate Division in Hackensack, NJ. In 1997 or 1998 I had little to do but study the back of his extremely orange head. At the end of the hour I had reached no firm opinion about what sits atop his scalp save one: it is not of this earth."

Pat English (Attorney): "Before the last election I wrote a story about Trump because it was of interest. It was going to be published in a legal publication but then CNN asked for it and then they actually did a number of interviews across the country. And then it got spiked. So, it never actually appeared in print."

Question: Why do you think your story got spiked?

Pat English: "I have no idea. Either did the reporter who did all the interviews."

Question: What was the premise of the feature story about Trump?

Pat English: "That he's a shit. You can quote me on that."

Question: Do you have proof to back that assertion?

Pat English: "Do I have proof!? [laughs uproariously] You can quote me on that laugh! Give me your email, I will send the story. When he was building the casinos in Atlantic City he defaulted on many contracts. His theory was...tell them you're not gonna pay, come up with a cock 'n bull story as to why. And ultimately settle for fifty cents on the dollar because he had more legal power than they do. And he put a lot of mom and pop businesses, construction businesses, glaziers, roofers, he put 'em out of business. Killed 'em."

Question: 80's?

Pat English: "Yeah. And early 90's."

Rick Glaser (Boxing matchmaker): "It was at the Lennox Lewis–Andrew Golota fight in Atlantic City. I was at the pre-fight party. He was standing right next to me. I said hello. We were talking about who we liked in the fight. He said to me, So who does the guy in the sunglasses like? I said, It doesn't matter who he fights, you can't bet against Lennox Lewis. He doesn't win all the time but when he does he makes it look easy. After the fight, which Lewis won by first round knockout, Trump walked up to me and said, That was a good call. And I said, It wasn't very difficult, downplaying my prediction. That's my story!"

Dan C. Weil (Journalist):

Question: How did you get the opportunity to interview Donald Trump?

Dan C. Weil: "I spoke to him twice about a house he bought in Palm Beach for around $40 million and then sold for $90+ million. I talked to him for Palm Beach Daily Business Review when he bought it (2004 or 2005) and The Real Deal, a New York City real estate publication, when he sold it, 2008, I believe."

"The first time we spoke, I couldn't decide whether to call him Donald, which is what I would usually do, or Mr. Trump, so I simply didn't say his name. Later I read that he expects to be called Mr. Trump. I didn't like that, so when I spoke to him the second time, I said "Hi Donald." He apparently wasn't pleased with that. He snapped back at me: "Does that publication make any money?" I wanted to defuse things, so I said with a friendly tone, "That's a good question. I don't know. I guess they can't be doing too badly, they have enough to pay me.""

"The first time we spoke, he repeatedly emphasized to me that this home he had purchased is the nicest property in Florida outside Mar-A-Lago. Then he asked me for affirmation that it is indeed the nicest. I figured best to be polite, so I said yes. The second time we spoke came after he had sold the house to a Russian oligarch. I asked him what it was like dealing with Russians. He said he liked it very much, because they're very straight forward, making negotiations easy."

Question: Did Trump strike you as a likable, charming person? Did you vote for him?

Dan C. Weil: "In general, he was quite friendly. I assume he spoke to me because it was good publicity for him. No comment on the vote. But I'm proud to say I voted for Obama twice."

Question: When you first called his office and spoke to his secretary about the interview and he called you back the same day?

Dan C. Weil: "Yes, each time I spoke to his secretary Rona, who was very nice."

Melvin "Doc" Stanley (Sports Media, NYC): "Donald
was both a boxing guy, hell still is, and always was
always great with me. Interviews, autographs. He and
Don King brought boxing back and to the east coast
down in Atlantic City. In fact the last time I saw him (in
New York City) he was with Mark Cuban and he stopped
to do an interview with me like always. And when I
asked him when was he and Don King going to get back
together and bring boxing back, he stopped and smiled
and told me to tell Cuban that and another person he
had with him. He really appreciated and liked the
comment."

Andrew Golota (Former Heavyweight boxer): "Trump came into my dressing room before the fight with Michael Grant (1999 at Trump Taj Mahal in Atlantic City). But it was so long ago I don't remember what we talked about [smiles]."

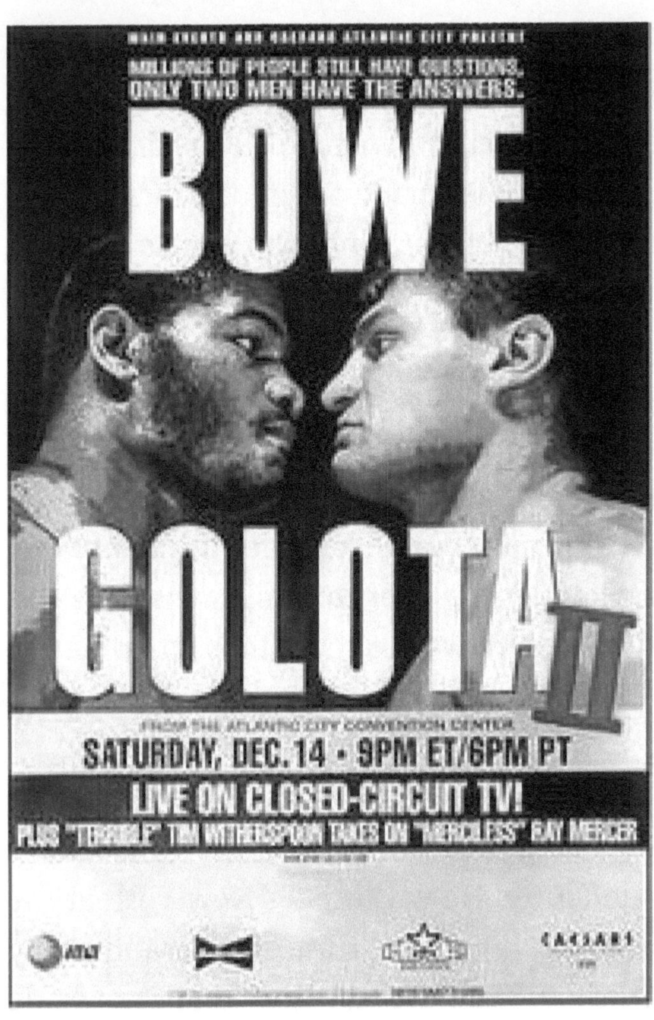

MAIN EVENTS AND CAESARS ATLANTIC CITY PRESENT
MILLIONS OF PEOPLE STILL HAVE QUESTIONS.
ONLY TWO MEN HAVE THE ANSWERS.
BOWE
GOLOTA II
FROM THE ATLANTIC CITY CONVENTION CENTER
SATURDAY, DEC. 14 • 9PM ET/6PM PT
LIVE ON CLOSED-CIRCUIT TV!
PLUS "TERRIBLE" TIM WITHERSPOON TAKES ON "MERCILESS" RAY MERCER
AT&T
CAESARS

Jim Tarsy (Wall Street, Bear Stearns Wealth Management for 47 years): "I went to a Knicks game at Madison Square Garden. We had very good seats, five or six rows from the court. Center. And who comes walking down...it was Trump and Marla Maples. I guess they were married at the time. They were sitting in the front row watching the game. And she's like off to the side. And all the sudden I see his phone rings. She answers it and she go over to him, as if to say, Do you want to talk to such and such? I remember he kept getting telephone calls and she kept going over to him, saying, Do you want to talk? And there were a few times when he did talk"

Question: Pretty busy guy. Always working on deals?

Jim Tarsy: "Evidently. He was Mister New York at the time. He was building the Trump Tower and many different Trump hotels. He was busy and everybody knew in New York. We're going back a lot of years. His parents were friends with my wife's parents. From Great Neck, that area, near Manhasset. My wife went to the Christian school and the two Trumps – the one that died from alcohol, but his sister belonged there. She's now a judge. But they were always helpful with the school and everything. My wife always has good feelings about Trump."

"I worked at Bear Stearns. I remember Trump would call Ace Greenberg (Bear Stearns CEO from 1978–1993 and Chairman of the Board 1985–2001) at the office every morning asking about his stocks."

Mario Costa (Boxing manager): "Matthew Hilton was fighting Robert Hines at the Las Vegas Hilton in November 1988. Matthew Hilton, up to that date, was undefeated as an amateur - he was about 102-0 with 98 knockouts and 29-0 as a pro. He never lost a match, amateur or pro. He became IBF Junior Middleweight champion of the world by beating Buster Drayton in Montreal when he was 21. Before the fight with Hines, Matthew had a dislocated rib, not bruised but dislocated. The main event was Michael Nunn against Juan Domingo Roldan. Matthew was going to pull out with the rib injury but decided not to. In the first and second rounds Matthew had Hines bloodied and down twice and out on his feet, hanging on the ropes. Hines came back and Matthew had trouble breathing and throwing his left hand. Hines won the decision. It was Matthew's first loss as a pro or amateur. For some reason Donald Trump came to see the fight. Maybe because Trump was Scottish and we had met Trump in Atlantic City at a Mike Tyson undercard. Trump liked Matthew, both were Scottish. I don't know why exactly Trump was there but he was there."

"After the fight Matthew was devastated. We were all devastated. Only me and Jimmy Murray were in the dressing room after. The dressing room was in a trailer in the back-parking lot of the Hilton. Matthew's dad was upset, he went somewhere. I left the trailer to get something for Matthew, his head was hurting. He was devastated. Jimmy stayed with Matthew. I came back. Somebody knocked on the door. Jimmy opened it, it was Donald Trump. Trump came to the trailer and wanted to talk to Matthew. Jimmy said, Matt, it's Donald Trump. Matthew said, 'Okay, let him in.' He came in. He kneeled down on one knee to talk with Matthew."

Jimmy Murray (Boxing cornerman): "Matthew Hilton lost the title to Robert "Bam Bam" Hines in 1988 in Las Vegas. I didn't even know Donald Trump was at the fight. After the fight, we went back to our trailer along the back of the Hilton. We used that for our dressing room. Everybody left. I sat there with Matthew, who was still in his robe. He sat in a folding chair; he was crying a little bit. He took a beating. We sat for a half hour. And who opens the door? Donald Trump. He came over and kneeled next to Matthew and said, 'Sorry to see you lost tonight. You're a young guy. Get back in the gym and you can get the belt back.' He patted him on the knee and said, 'Hope to see you back in Atlantic City.' And then he left. The bodyguard was standing outside the door."

"I also met Donald Trump in January 1988 when Mike Tyson fought Larry Holmes in Atlantic City. Tyson knocked Holmes out in the fourth round. Holmes made $3 million for that night. I was backstage in the dressing room with Davey Hilton, who fought on the undercard that night against Hector Rosario. We were right next to Tyson. We saw Trump come up, Don Johnson, Arnold Schwarzeneggar's wife. They all came to see Mike. The next day me and Mario and old Davey Hilton went to Don King's office, then to Trump's office at the Trump

Plaza Hotel. We were in the office sitting with Donald. Trump told the former football player member of his entourage to set up a table for Matthew Hilton and his people for the party he was throwing that night Muhammad Ali, for his 47th birthday. I remember the one guy was complaining to Donald about something in his room and Donald told him, 'We'll try to do better next time.' We were invited to the party, three hundred invited guests, we went there, table of ten with Matthew Hilton. Donald Trump's first wife was there. That was a good time by all."

"Another time, on a Sunday afternoon a year later in 1989, there was a boxing card at the Ballroom of Convention Center Boardwalk Hall. We went on a Sunday afternoon. We were sitting in the second row. Before the main event, Donald and his bodyguard, were walking to the door to go back to the Plaza Hotel. He spotted Matthew Hilton, turned around and came back and shook hands with him. Donald always tried to do good for Matthew. He liked Matthew. Matthew was a likable guy."

Chris Kotsopolous (Former New York Ranger and NHL defenseman): "Yes I met Trump but I'm not going to divulge anything, sorry. I love Trump."

CHRIS KOTSOPOULOS
1980-81

Roscoe Tanner (Tennis Champion): "I stayed in Mar A Lago. He and Michael Milliken had a fundraiser for prostate cancer. We would go and play tennis with men who paid to play with us in a Pro-Am. He personally invited me. We stayed on the grounds. He's actually not a bad tennis player. He plays it like an athlete would play it, he doesn't back down. I remember he hosted parties. Always a very good guy, normal guy. But he's not gonna hold back. That's pretty nice to see. He's very likable, I have no problems with him."

Barry Beck (Former New York Ranger and NHL defenseman): "None that I can discuss Scoop. Met almost everyone in New York through the early eighties. Sorry."

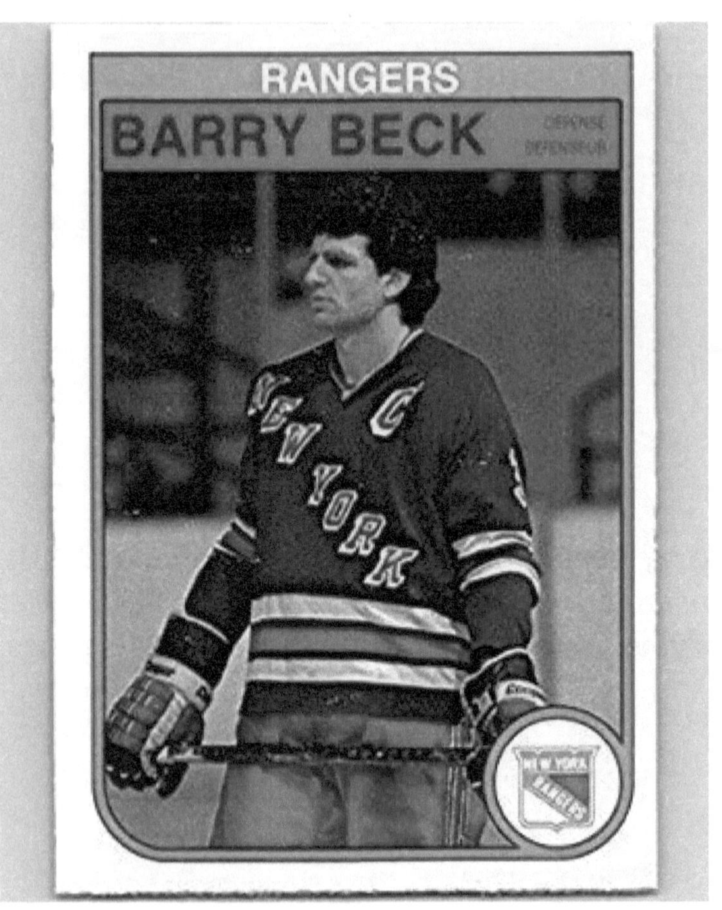

RANGERS
BARRY BECK
DÉFENSE
DEFENSEUR
NEW YORK
C
NEW YORK
RANGERS

Micheal Marley (New York Post sports columnist): "I met Donald and Ivana in Atlantic City about five or six times, covering boxing events in the 1980s. Once when she was there and he was not. They always said the same thing, 'Enjoy yourself.' I thought to myself.... if I had their money, I would do that in style."

Gary Cohn (Former Top Economic Advisor for President Trump): "It has been an honor to serve my country and enact pro-growth economic policies to benefit the American people, in particular the passage of historic tax reform. I am grateful to the President for giving me this opportunity and wish him and the Administration great success in the future."

Larry Barnes (Former Welterweight title challenger, top contender): "He always gave me what I needed. I never had a problem with Mr. Trump. Now he's President. I just want to say good luck to him in the White House. That's it. I met him vaguely, very vaguely, at a press conference in Atlantic City before my fight with Felix Trinidad. He was a very nice gentleman. As the President, it's another story - I don't know him as the President now but I know him as a boxing promoter. I fought for the world title against Felix Trinidad at Convention Center. I don't know if he was there watching - I was thinking about Felix Trinidad. But you know what? I wish the President all the luck in the world, I wish him the best. And I wish he stops getting a lot of bad press because I really care about Donald Trump."

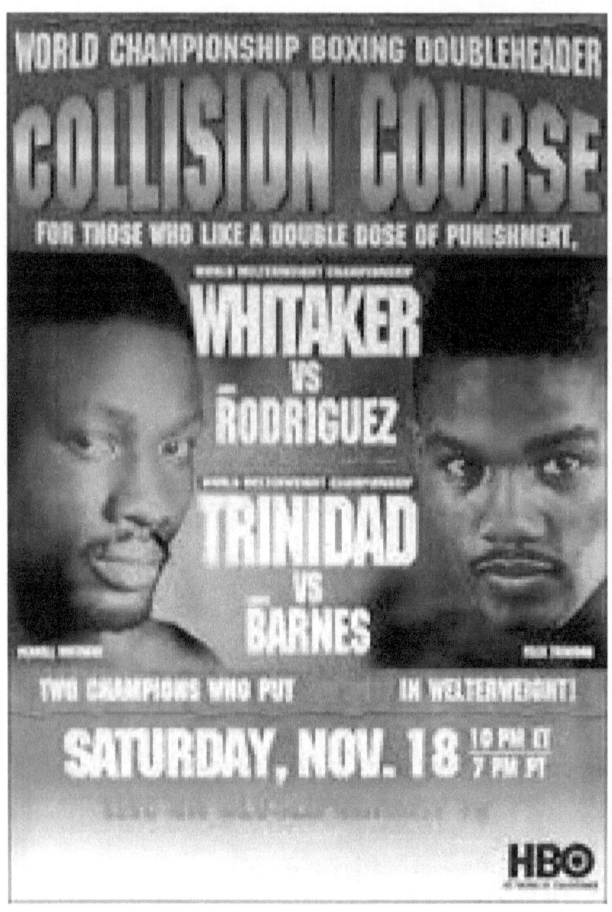

WORLD CHAMPIONSHIP BOXING DOUBLEHEADER
COLLISION COURSE
FOR THOSE WHO LIKE A DOUBLE DOSE OF PUNISHMENT.
WHITAKER
VS
RODRIGUEZ
TRINIDAD
VS
BARNES
SATURDAY, NOV. 18
10 PM ET
7 PM PT
HBO

Randy Walker (Tennis Publisher): "October 2014, weeks after he announced he was running for President. I was invited to a corporate golf outing for Turkish Airlines, the Turkish Airlines World Golf Cup, which is a global amateur golf event. Winners of the regional events qualify for international finals in Turkey in conjunction with Turkish Airlines European Tour Golf event. Great promotion. This was at Trump National Golf Club in Bedminster, NJ. The person who invited me the last couple of years was Ben Sturner, who is the CEO of Leverage Agency. So we had a wonderful time at the event. Ben knows my propensity for tweeting. He said, you've got to tweet something @tennispublisher out this weekend and tag @realdonaldtrump because he's totally gonna retweet you. So I was thinking to tweet something interesting and compelling."

"So we're playing the golf course. I really enjoyed the golf course though I didn't play great, I had a few good holes. We went from the ninth green to the tenth tee - you had to go through the parking lot to get to the back nine. You go through where the outdoor grill is. All the chefs are out there. Steaks, burgers, chicken on the grill. It smelled really awesome. Okay, I gotta have one of these hamburgers. I'm a plain hamburger guy, lettuce, tomato. The chef fixed it right up, took a bite and my mouth just started salivating. I thought: This is the best hamburger I've ever had in my life. Delicious. Five bites over with delicious."

"Finished the golf. Okay, I gotta get a tweet out. I said, The best part of Donald Trump's Bedminster National course was not only the great golf but I also had the best hamburger that I ever had in my life. So that was my tweet that I was going to put out at my buddy's urging. And then sure enough, within an hour, I look at my phone and it says @realdonaldtrump retweeted your tweet [laughs]. It's kind of a funny story that I like to tell. And I either get a high five or a frown and somebody turns away and ignores me. It's a good cocktail party story, right?"

(Yes!)

Joe Abba (Musician) "I met Trump backstage at the Taj Mahal, where I was playing with Jessical Simpson. We were told not to speak to him unless spoken to. I didn't care. Went up and shook his hand. We were all talking and he kept reaching into a bus pan filled with drinks for the band. Little bottles of soda and water. He would open one, take a sip, close it, put it back. Then, grab a different one, open it, take a sip, put it back. Must've opened about five of them over ten minutes. Completely wasteful. Typical rich guy bullshit."

Question: What did he talk about?

Joe Abba: "Not much. He was just chatting with Jessica Simpson and that clown Omarosa was there too. It was for filming the final episode of the first season of The Apprentice. It was all fake reality TV nonsense. Omarosa was pretending to be running the whole thing and Trump was just trying to get face time with Simpson. Melania was there. They had just gotten married. She was standing there with that squinty facial expression she always makes. He was dismissive at best of all of us. Which is why when I was told not to speak to Mr. Trump unless he speaks to you, I went right up to him and shook his hand (laughs). This was in 2004"

IRRESISTIBLE JESSICA SIMPSON

Nick Kish (Former Director of Football Operations for USFL team Jacksonville Bulls): "I was working for the Jacksonville Bulls when Donald Trump owned the New Jersey Generals team. We drafted the Heisman Trophy winner Doug Flutie. I got a call from the USFL office in New York, saying I could not draft Flutie because Trump wanted the rights to Flutie. Trump wanted Flutie for the Generals, to play with another Heisman Trophy winner Herschel Walker. So myself and (General Manager) Larry Csonka ended up trading the rights to Flutie for another quarterback, Brian Sipe, who was an MVP player for the Cleveland Browns. As part of the agreement, Trump agreed to pay three-quarters of Sipe's salary of I think it was $900,000, which turned out to be around $700,000 a year. Trump expected our team to lay down and give him Flutie for nothing. It ended up working out well for everybody. We got a good quarterback, they got Flutie."

"The league lasted from 1983-1985. It was Trump who screwed it up, otherwise it may have kept going. Trump convinced the USFL owners that the NFL would absorb about half the teams in the USFL if we stopped playing in the spring and moved to the fall in 1986 to compete directly with the NFL. I was at the meeting of owners and general managers in Amelia Island, Florida when Trump stood up and convinced all the owners to do this. The USFL filed an antitrust lawsuit against the National Football League in 1986, and a jury ruled that the NFL had violated anti-monopoly laws. However, in a victory in name only, the USFL was awarded a judgment of just $1, which under antitrust laws, was tripled to $3. This court decision effectively ended the USFL's existence. (The league never played its planned 1986 season, and by the time it folded, it had lost over $163 million - over $381 million in 2019 dollars)."

"When Trump owned the Generals in the USFL, that was when he got his first notoriety around the country. The notoriety of sports and his involvement with that team had a tremendous impact on his notoriety nationwide. Up until 1983-84, he was one of many wealthy real estate developers. He parlayed the football thing into a lot of recognition."

Question: Lasting memory of Donald Trump?

Nick Kish: "My son was the same age as his son. When he would come to Jacksonville for games with his first wife and his three sons, my son would hang out with his kids up in the skybox. I would say he was little arrogant back then. He was used to getting things his way. That's the way he was. Not saying it as a negative thing. He developed his power, he knew it and he used it in real estate, sports. He decided he wanted to be President of the United States and he was able to do it. Not a lot of people can do that."

1985 New Jersey Generals
TRI-STATE Ford DEALERS
TRI-STATE Ford DEALERS

Iran Barkley (Former Middleweight and Super Middleweight champion): "I met Donald Trump when me and Roberto Duran fought (in 1989). I met him there in Atlantic City, he was saying, 'Great fight, I never saw a fight like your's. You guys were going to battle.' I know him from his hotels in Atlantic City. I saw him coming through his hotels or when he sees me, we talk, sometimes we wave and stuff."

Chris Alderucci (Golf nut): "I played one round of golf with Trump (at Trump National Golf Course in Bedminster, NJ) years before he became President. I never got a word in the whole day. It was basically him talking, us listening. He is a decent golfer with a good foot wedge [laughs]."

Randy Neumann (Former heavyweight boxer and pro boxing referee): "In Atlantic City I met him. He's pretty tall. I remember being in the elevator with him. He's bigger than me."

TRUMP
PLAZA
TRUMP PLAZA

Vijay Amritraj (Tennis Champion, Actor, Commentator, Talk Show Host, United Nations Ambassador for peace): "Yes I did meet Donald Trump a few years ago, right before he ran for President (2012). He was a guest on my TV show (Louis Philippe DIMENSIONS on CNN-IBN). I did a one-on-one interview with him for an hour. I spent a whole morning with him in his office in New York City."

Question: Any standout memories from the experience?

Vijay Amritraj: "He's a huge sports fan. He had seen me play a lot of my matches. He commented on my matches. The interview was very easy for me because he's a huge tennis fan and golf fan. He played some tennis as a kid and he continues to play golf. For me it was an easy conversation. I could literally ask him about anything. Because he was a big fan of sports. We also talked about The Apprentice and business."

Question: How long did it take to score the face to face TV interview with Donald Trump? Was it a fairly quick process?

Vijay Amritraj: "Yes Scoop. I left a message at his office and he called me back right away."

Vinny Pazienza (Former three-time world champion boxer): "I didn't just meet Donald Trump, I made millions for our President! I made Donald Trump millions of dollars. Donald Trump loves me. I made him, literally, that's no joke, I made the President of our country millions of dollars. I'm glad. And so far I like what he's doing with him being the President. At first everyone was skeptical but I think he's gonna be the best President we ever had."

Question: Which fights did you fight under Trump casino property?

Vinny Pazienza: "I fought a lot of fights with Trump. A lot of fights - Hector Camacho, Greg Haugen, Roberto Duran, Roy Jones, so many fights. I fought in Atlantic City a lot."

Question: Remember any words Trump said to you?

Vinny Pazienza: "He was always nice. He was always cool. We hung out. He never tried to give me advice on anything. He was very cool. And nice with me all the time. I'd be nice to somebody too if they made me millions of dollars [laughs]. But he was cool."

Kirk Lang (Photographer): "I have photos with tons of celebrities: Reese Witherspoon, Jim Brown, Rev. Jesse Jackson, Derek Jeter, etc. However, my photo collection was always missing something – a picture with a President. I got jealous in the early 2000s when my mom's best's friend's son, attending Housatonic Community College, got a picture with Bill Clinton during his visit to the campus. I thought about maybe catching Jimmy Carter during a book signing, but most often at a book signing, they don't pose they just sign. I used to work for town newspapers in Fairfield and Westport and thought of reaching out to a Clinton friend or two who lives in Westport. However, in about 2009 or 2010 I managed to catch a photo with Donald Trump outside Trump International Hotel. I get a photo with Trump, his daughter Ivanka and his wife Melania all at the same time. Never in a million years did I imagine that six or seven years later that photo with Trump would become my Presidential photo, the elusive picture I had been missing. The night of the election in 2016, when Trump was going against Hillary Clinton, I actually went to bed a little early for once, a rare thing for me. When I hit the hay, Hilary was showing an early lead against Trump in the race to the White House. I said to myself, 'oh well it's looking like I'll still be without a presidential photo.' Later that night, I wake up around 10:30 p.m. And lo and behold, Trump is our next Presidential of the United States. I'll be honest. I'm not a fan of the guy. I voted for Hillary, but somewhere in the back of my mind I sort of hoped he would win, for that one selfish reason."

Question: Was it spontaneous that you got your photo opp with Trump?

Kirk Lang: "I came close to getting photos with Trump twice before, but had no friend with me to snap the shot. He briefly stopped before getting in his limo the night of Holyfield-Lewis (Madison Square Garden.) and then I almost got him at Don King's roast at the Hilton. That second time. I asked a stranger, if I ask Trump for a photo and he stops, can you take the picture? So, Trump does come out, I hand the camera to my new friend, but he doesn't take the photo in time before Trump gets on the escalator to go to the floor below. I ran into Trump unexpectedly at his hotel/tower near the corner of Central Park and Columbus Circle. I had no clue I would run into him that day. And yet that day I got not only Trump but also his wife and daughter."

Lloyd Carroll (Columnist at Queens Chronicle weekly newspaper): "I was at an NBC press conference for The Apprentice. His first season had done very well. He was there with his assistant George, the Jewish guy, I forget his last name, and his whole staff. And I go over to Trump and introduce myself. One of the girls on the show was from Philadelphia, my old neck of the woods. She had a very whiny, Brooklyn accent. Her name was Holly. So I go over to Trump and I tell him, 'Donald, I love The Apprentice, but one of your contestants, Holly, with her deez, dem, doz, she should have been on the Lefrak Apprentice.' Samuel Lefrak was the poor man's Trump, doing middle class housing, Lefrak City in Queens, rent control, things regulated. So Trump said, 'Holly's a very nice girl....' Then he tapped me on the shoulder (and added), 'But I know what you mean [laughs]!'"

"And I wrote about that encounter. And I sent a copy to Howard Rubinstein, who is Trump's PR guy. And one thing about Trump is he reads everything. Any time is name is anywhere, he reads where it's from. Oh, but another story, following up that. After the success of The Apprentice, he was being roasted at The Friar's Club. It might have been a year later. So I was covering it. So at the press conference I raise my hand.

Trump was doing his shtick... I've seen grown men cry at these roasts. I raise my hand. I asked, 'Donald, the fact you grew up in Jamaica Estates Queens, is that an advantage, you have a tougher skin, you can handle this better other can?' He said, 'Being from Queens is always an advantage.'"

"I wrote that up. Sent that to the Queens Chronicle. I sent it to Howard Rubinstein. Rubinstein must have shown it to Trump. A year later I'm at Trump Tower. The state of Virginia was having a wine event there. Bob McDonald, who got in trouble later, was the governor. Trump sees me, taps me on the shoulder, 'What's new in Queens?' I said, 'Not much Donald, we miss you.'"

"So that's my Donald Trump stories. I saw he was just at The Friar's Club two days ago. And I saw photos of Trump back in the day. I think he had more fun. I absolutely feel he had more fun before he became President Trump than he is now. He was young, he was having the time of his life. I always wonder if he has regrets about becoming President."

Bobby Czyz (Former Light Heavyweight and Cruiserweight boxing champion): "I actually almost worked for Donald Trump. I fought for and defended world titles in his casinos in Atlantic City. Then I retired briefly for six months in 1989 and I almost worked for him. But then I came out of retirement to fight again and won two more world titles."

Question: He offered you a job?

Bobby Czyz: "It would have been as one of his representatives in his casino."

Question: Memories of meeting him?

Bobby Czyz: "What I was most impressed about Donald was when he said something, he meant it. He meant it. And eventually it would come true. And I thought that was pretty interesting. I didn't think he had the chance to win the Presidency because of the Clinton conspiracy. Look, I know they're all crooked. So many people died under the Clinton regime that it doesn't make sense. But Donald beat her. He signed on to a position he doesn't need to win. I love the guy. I

think he's incredible. And I'm happy he's our
President."

Question: Which fights of your's did he stage?

Bobby Czyz: "I had a couple of title defenses. I think
one was Willie Edwards in 1987. Then moving up to
cruiserweight at Taj Mahal against Robert Daniels in
1991. So at least two I had in his casinos. He was there
at the fight. I saw him a couple of times. But at fight
time your mind is blank. You don't recognize anything.
I know he was there at one of them but I believe he
was at both. And there were after-fight parties.
Sometimes he would show up to make his obligatory
presence. Good guy. Good guy all the way around. I like
the guy and he got my vote. And he'll get it again."

FULL-COLOR PINUP OF SUGAR RAY LEONARD
$2.25 / $2.75 Canada
14427 Sept. 1987
The Knockout Boxing Magazine
KO
MARK BRELAND
Charting His Course To Superstardom

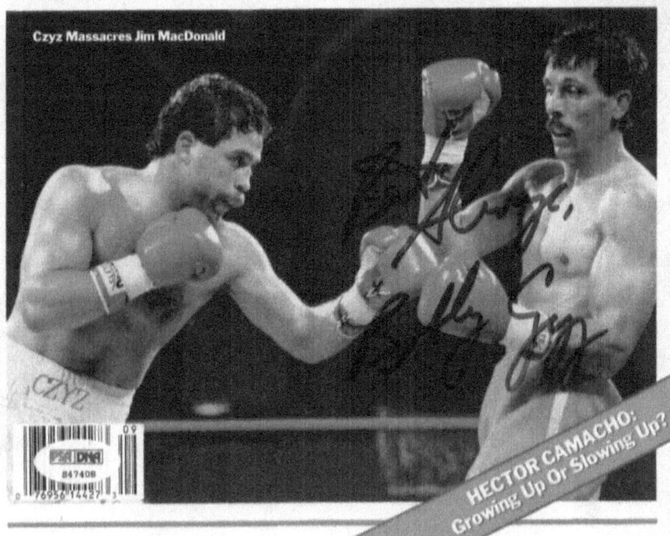

BOBBY CZYZ
Finally, His Accomplishments Match His Appeal
Czyz Massacres Jim MacDonald
HECTOR CAMACHO:
Growing Up Or Slowing Up?

Carling Bassett-Seguso (Former tennis pro): "The greatest moment of my career was the semifinals of the US Open. I think it might have been 1986 (actually 1984). Beating Hana Mandlikova. And my dad (John F. Bassett) was sitting in the box. And he was sitting with, of all people, Donald Trump. I loved the US Open. I love New York. I was just so happy."

XEROX
テレホンカード50

Jeff Freeman (Boxing journalist): "The first real live fight I ever attended as a fan was the 1993 Evander Holyfield–Alex Stewart rematch in Atlantic City. The fight was lame. The experience was legendary. I carpooled with two friends from Brockton, Edwin Ayala and F Peter Gaskins. We had regular seats up in the crowd but me being me, I had to get closer, so I told Ed I was going to walk around. He came with me. Peter stayed in his seat. I ran into Riddick Bowe, the world heavyweight champion. I asked him for an autograph. He said no. He asked me how tall I was. I told him. Then I headed us backstage. We saw ex-Tyson trainer Kevin Rooney and took a group photo with him. John John Molina's management team asked us to take a picture of them after he won on the undercard. Then a future President of the United States walked through the area by the dressing rooms. He strolled right by me as evidenced by his tightly cropped framing in the photo shot I took which was snapped with an old fashion flashbulb camera and developed at some random pharmacy or whatnot. I didn't talk to him. He didn't stop. Then we jumped into Vinny Pazienza's entourage for his ring walk to go fight Lloyd Honeyghan but got scared we'd end up in the ring so we broke it off. We never returned to our seats; instead meeting back up with Peter to watch the main event on the floor, close to where Holyfield's Olympic teammates and other fighters were gathering. Pernell Whitaker signed the back of my ticket. Michael Moorer got testy about being photographed."

Dave "The Koz" Kozlowski (Host of Inside Tennis with The Koz TV Show): "We did five or six interviews. The first one was at the Chris Evert Celebrity Pro-Am. We were posing together for photographers and one of the photographers asked,' Let me know when you're ready.' Donald said, 'Come over.' I was side by side with Donald. Right as they were about to shoot us, Donald stepped forward about six inches in front of us - he got closer to the cameras. I was not insulted. I was impressed by his skill, how he handled the media and got the maximum out of the media."

"I was able to develop a bit of a relationship with his right hand man, named Sal. I got to know him, he'd tell me when to come to the booth at the US Open we I could do a quick interview. One time at a night match at the US Open I had just arrived. And I didn't have my interview jacket on for that. So he arrived at the red carpet at the US Open. I asked for 30 seconds for a quick interview. He saw that I didn't have a jacket on and said, 'I'll catch you later.' I knew. He didn't want to do the interview with me if I didn't have my jacket on. Seconds later, guess who walks up? Dr. Phil. And we did it. So I didn't need a jacket for Dr. Phil. But Donald was very supportive of tennis and the Chris Evert organization. I

know he was in attendance when George Bush Sr. was there. That might be when they first met."
Question: Was Donald Trump a likable guy for you in your brief encounters with him?

Dave Kozlowski: "Yes. I think you have to earn his respect. If you have a bit of panache in yourself, if you say something cool or react cool to what he says, he will react to it. He's a cool guy. He carries himself well. He has an air about him. Panache. He's a proud man of his successes. He's not overly humble or narcissistic. You know he wasn't lacking self-esteem or confidence. He has the demeanor of one of the biggest men in the world in business. He knows that. How he handles himself."

Koz interviews American tennis star Tennys Sandgren.

Montell Griffin (Former light heavyweight champion): "I met Donald Trump twice - Lennox Lewis fight with Tommy Morrison in Atlantic City. I was at that fight and I was in his dressing room. Trump came in there and talked with everybody. And then in 1997 when I fought Roy Jones at Trump Taj Mahal. He came in there and shook my hand, said congratulations on winning your title in my hotel. And I got a picture of it. So it's much respect. When he talked with me personally, it meant a lot to me."

LIVE AT THE TRUMP TAJ MAHAL
"THE BATTLE OF THE UNDEFEATED"
WBC LIGHT-HEAVYWEIGHT CHAMPIONSHIP
ROY JONES, JR VS MONTELL GRIFFIN
FRIDAY, MARCH 21, 1997
Plus exciting undercard bouts featuring Olympic Gold Medalist David Reid!
Official Program
TRUMP TAJ MAHAL
In Association With Square Ring, Inc. And Cedric Kushner Promotions

Richard Pagliaro (Journalist): "I have two witnesses to this story so Trump can't call it Fake News. It happened before a Jimmy Connors match at Manhattanville College in Purchase in the 1990s. Trump inhaled two dogs faster than King Kong swallowing a couple of tic tacs."

Artwork by NYC based artist Michael Saviello.

Micky Ward (Former Boxing Champion): "Without getting into politics, I met Donald years ago when I fought at the Trump Plaza, the Harrah's Trump, all his hotels. He's a very good guy. He loves boxing. He's a big boxing fan. And uh, I like him. You know what it is? He says what everyone's thinking. That's why some people don't like him. It's okay if you don't like what I like. Me personally, I like him."

Savannah Gray (Restaurant hostess, Bradenton, FL): "Daytona 500 February 16th, 2020. About three months prior to my family's Trump encounter at the Daytona 500, we were just talking about race car driving and the fun experience we had at the Atlanta speedway. I brought up the idea that we should go see the Daytona 500 since we now live back in Florida and my grandpa and nana were visiting from Minnesota - my grandpa LOVES NASCAR. My parents decided we should do it because of the perfect timing and the thrill of the racing and patriotic experience that we enjoyed from the Atlanta motor speedway. We had no idea that Trump was going to be there until three days prior to the race. The first thing I heard when I woke up on Friday the 14th was that Trump was going to be showing up to the race! Wow, I honestly could not believe it because I would have never thought this could happen to me and my family. We had no idea what to expect because this was new to us. We had no idea if he was going to be physically present to the audience or what? Well, we were in for a huge surprise! When we got there, we got VIP passes to see the race car drivers in the grass/track area. There was a great crowd of people, very patriotic and full of energy. My family and I were just walking around enjoying the sights, and then we heard this gentleman on a microphone saying, 'Trump is taking a landing with his Air Force One plane.'"

"We watched him and his team in the plane and he did a fly-by around the stadium! I could not believe my eyes. I would have never thought in my life that I would be in the same area as Trump was, and his gorgeous wife Melania! I mean, even if you do not like the guy, which I believe no one in the audience disliked him whatsoever, at least you can say you got to see the President of the United States of America! That is impressive and very special. Trump continued to amaze us when we all took our seats for the national anthem. Melania and Trump, after the national anthem, walked up to a podium and he started to perform a speech for the NASCAR racers! Now I really can't believe my eyes! Trump is talking right in front of us! The best memory I will never forget was when the NASCAR drivers got into their vehicles and lined up by their pitstop stations. After Trump telling the drivers to be safe, he said, "NASCAR drivers, start your engines!" and simultaneously, the drivers turned on and revved their engines and the crowd goes wild shouting, "FOUR MORE YEARS! FOUR MORE YEARS! FOUR MORE YEARS!!!" After that, him and his team took a drive around the track in a black limo. My family was sitting in the first row of the stadium just before the finishing line, and we waved at him and he waved back to all of us! What a great experience. Days like these reminds me of how amazing it is to be an American citizen, and I appreciate this country and how far we have come!"

DAYTONA

About the cover artist: **Karin Billings** is an artist based in Sarasota, FL. In 1972 as Karin Schluter, she won an Olympic silver medal in Equestrian competing at the Munich Games. You can view her work at www.karinbillings.com

Liz Crokin (Journalist): "I worked in the mainstream media for many, many years and my goal as a mainstream media journalist, which is the goal of any mainstream media journalist, is not only to get the biggest story but the more salacious story is on a public figure, a celebrity or a politician, the better the story is gonna do. And the better your story does - that is how you move your way up the ladder in the field of journalism. I had the privilege of covering Donald Trump. I covered him in his show The Apprentice. And I also had the privilege of covering his family members. Over the years I would get some tips about President Trump that were salacious and they were good - if they were true. Every tip that I looked into, that had any dirt, didn't turn out to be true."

"And I was bummed because that would have elevated my career. A big, front page cover story on Donald Trump would have been a huge feather in my cap. So over the years covering President Trump, I was not able to get any dirt on this man. I found the opposite to be true, which is he is not a playboy billionaire, he's not a degenerate, he doesn't drink, he does not do alcohol and he's actually a very good, stand-up guy, who has a big heart, who does a lot of charity for many people over the years. We are living in unprecedented times right now and I did a video on my You Tube channel based on an article I wrote about him in 2016 to remind the world who President Trump really is."

"Let me tell you about what Donald Trump has done. President Trump will go through the newspaper and read stories about people who are dealing with tragedies. And he will clip out the stories and ask a secretary to find these people and he will help them. In 1986 Trump prevented the foreclosure of Annabelle Hill's family farm after her husband committed suicide. Trump was so moved by this story that he called the auction and he stopped the sale of her home and gave her money so she wouldn't have to lose her home. Those are the kinds of things that Trump has a history of doing for many, many, many years. But the mainstream media will never tell you of any of these stories."

"So how many times have we heard from the mainstream media that Trump is anti-Semitic? And he hates Jews? Let me tell you a story of what he did for a sick, little, Orthodox Jewish boy. In 1988 a commercial airline refused to fly Andrew Ten, a sick, Orthodox child with a rare illness, across the country to get medical care because he had to travel with an elaborate life support system. His parents contacted Trump for help. What did he do? He did not hesitate to send his plane to Los Angeles to take this little boy across the country to New York so he could get the medical care that he needed."

"In 2014, Trump gave $25,000 to Marine sargent Andrew Tahmooressi after he spent seven months in a Mexican jail for accidentally crossing the U.S.-Mexican border. President Barack Obama couldn't even be bothered to make a phone call to get the troubled Marine released. It was Trump who came to the rescue."

"Another story. In 2000, Trump happened to be watching the Maury Povich show and the episode featured a girl named Megan who suffered from a brittle bone disease. Trump called his friend Maury Povich and gave money for Megan to help her medical care. Another story you won't hear in the mainstream media happened in 1995. His limousine broke down on the Garden State Parkway while driving to Atlantic City. A husband and wife pulled over to help fix the limousine. A week later the husband and wife received a deed to their home, paid off. Did you know that in 1996 Trump filed a lawsuit against the city of Palm Beach, Florida for discrimination against his Mar-A-Lago club because his club allowed Jews and blacks. Still think he's racist?"

"In 2008 the singer Jennifer Hudson's family members were tragically murdered in Chicago. When President Trump found out about this, he called her and told her he would put her up in his Trump Tower hotel in Chicago and cover all the costs. And not only did he do that, he also provided extra security for her and her family during this time."

"I'd encourage people to be very cautious about anything the mainstream media puts out. Ask yourself, Do you really think President Trump is a racist? Do you really think that so many conservatives who support Trump are racist? Do you really think that race is that big of an issue - or is it an issue that's being driven by the mainstream media to divide us? I encourage people to use discernment and listen to your heart and think about these things. And ignore the fake news."

 Mark "Scoop" Malinowski has authored the following books. He is based in Teaneck, NJ and Bradenton Beach, FL.

Marcelo Rios: The Man We Barely Knew

Heavy Armageddon: The Tyson vs. Lewis Championship Battle

Facing Federer

Facing Nadal

Facing Hewitt

Facing McEnroe

Facing Sampras

Facing Andy Murray

Facing Marat Safin

Facing Serena Williams/Steffi Graf (Double Book)

The Book of Joy

Facing Bob Probert: Portrait of a Hockey Legend

Muhammad Ali: Portrait of a Champion

He is currently working on:

Facing Guillermo Vilas

LeRoy Neiman: Portrait of the Artist